CONSTRUCTION WORK

JOSÉE DUBEAU / LORRAINE GILBERT / JINNY YU

SANDRA DYCK, CURATOR / WITH AN ESSAY BY PETRA HALKES

CARLETON UNIVERSITY ART GALLERY

FOREWORD

Construction Work brings together for the first time the work of three artists who, individually, are familiar to audiences in the Ottawa-Gatineau region, Josée Dubeau, Lorraine Gilbert, and Jinny Yu. Although they work in different media – Yu is a painter, Dubeau a sculptor, and Gilbert a photographer – this grouping makes evident their unsuspected commonality: a shared passion for ideas of space, place, and the built environment. Building on the striking blend of fact and fiction in Lorraine Gilbert's new photographic series *Le Patrimoine*, which depicts the levelling influence of globalization on familiar icons of the rural Québec landscape, Josée Dubeau and Jinny Yu have created new works that engage CUAG's architecture. Recalling the architecture of such avatars of twentieth-century Modernism as Le Corbusier and Ray and Charles Eames, Yu's austere wall painting *Sequence* and Dubeau's playful construction *Life in a Kite* take the theme of the constructed environment beyond the local into abstract and symbolic realms.

Guest writer Petra Halkes has contributed a penetrating essay that situates the exhibition theme and the individual artists' works in relation to the notion of 'de-construction', which the influential French philosopher Jacques Derrida used to critique the stability of theoretical constructions of autonomous identities, whether of institutions, disciplines, beliefs, or gender. She argues that an underlying longing for harmony can be found in Gilbert's photographs, Yu's wall painting, and Dubeau's construction. Recognizing the constructivist impulse they share, she finds that they "have sifted through the rubble of Modernist and Romantic dreams to discover desires that remain undemolished; these they set into new constructions, where they can be re-examined for their utopian value."

I would like to thank Jinny Yu, Lorraine Gilbert, and Josée Dubeau for their many contributions to this project, not least the beautiful and intelligent works of art they produced for the exhibition. My thanks go also to the exhibition's curator, Sandra Dyck, for her excellent research and expert coordination of the exhibition and publication; to Patrick Lacasse for his efficient assistance with the framing and installation; and to Kelsey Blackwell for her sensitive catalogue design, which gives visual form to the themes of the exhibition. Finally, I wish to acknowledge the generous support of Carleton University, the Canada Council for the Arts, and the Ontario Arts Council.

DIANA NEMIROFF
Director

CONSTRUCTION WORK

PETRA HALKES

Harmony reigning over all things, regulating all the things of our lives,
is the spontaneous, indefatigable and tenacious quest of man animated by a single force:
the sense of the divine, and pursuing one aim: to make a paradise on earth.
LE CORBUSIER[i]

Construction Work, the title of this exhibition, conjures up images of growling machines, stacks of lumber, and piles of debris navigated by muscled men and women. Instead, a dreamy lightness pervades the works of all three artists. Josée Dubeau's installation, a scale model of a late-Modernist house, seems made of air, drawn with rectangular modules made of delicate pine rods high into the three-dimensional space of the gallery. Airy, too, is Jinny Yu's wall painting, composed of thin bands of grey on white and reaching up to the mezzanine level of the gallery. There, they touch a frieze painted on aluminium panels, depicting sheets of papers scattered by the wind. Lorraine Gilbert's black and white photographs construct fairy-tale fantasies of the Québec countryside. When here, at last, we find a real bulldozer in a sandpit, it is so small it appears toy-like and shares space with sunbathers who use the gravel quarry as a beach (*Sunbathers*, 2006).

Clearly, the exhibition's title refers not only to building with materials, but to the more intangible construction of theoretical frameworks. Such frameworks, built upon observations and interpretations of cultural processes that seem wholly immaterial, are always communicated – made *manifest* – through representation, which includes not only words but the signs and symbols of images, of architecture, and of the landscape. By touching on both meanings of the word *construction*, then, the exhibition provides a site in which to contemplate how our material world – the landscape as well as the built environment – is shaped by the seemingly immaterial forces of individual and collective dreams, desires and beliefs.

Curator Sandra Dyck underscored the ideational links between the works by creating a visual flow from one artist's work to the next. Each accommodated in its own distinct space, the three installations echo and exchange the desires they are built on. They invite us to let our feet draw the lines between them. We weave in and out of Dubeau's installation *Life in a Kite* (2009), our eyes tracing the outlines of furniture and walls of this "building" that was inspired by a famous 1949 Case Study House in Los Angeles, the Eames House.[ii] A similar Modernist precision is present in the rhythmic, vertical lines of Yu's *Sequence* (2009), which mimic a fenestration pattern in Le Corbusier's Dominican Monastery of Sainte-Marie de La Tourette, near Lyon, France (1953–57).[iii] Following these soaring lines, our gaze meets a chaotic scene of flying papers in a panoramic painting, which we can examine more closely

Previous pages and opposite: Lorraine Gilbert, *Sunbathers*, 2006 (details)

by climbing the stairs to the gallery's mezzanine. Returning downstairs, we wander off into Gilbert's photographic landscapes, a series entitled *Le Patrimoine* [Heritage], which invite us to contemplate the randomness of nature and our amusing, but not harmless, attempts to create order from it.

There are, no doubt, many interpretations to be made from this interweaving of three artists' works. My own reading of *Construction Work* focuses on the persistence of the human desire to create a utopian place of harmony. Such a paradise, in which all contingencies, including those of our own inadequate existence, would be dissolved, is not a real possibility, as we all know. But the better life in a castle-in-the-sky remains a powerful incentive to reimagine life's possibilities here and now. The artists in this exhibition have sifted through the rubble of Modernist and Romantic dreams to discover desires that remain undemolished; these they set into new constructions, where they can be reexamined for their utopian value.

Coining the word "*de*-construction" in 1967, the philosopher Jacques Derrida set out to show that theoretical constructions of autonomous identities, whether of institutions, disciplines, beliefs, or gender, are always deconstructed from within.[iv] Like buildings erected in material space, they are only as solid as the ground they stand on. No matter how indestructible an edifice appears, it remains dependent on a foundation that touches the living and shifting amalgam of the planet's geo-structure: it is affected by the earth's hidden fissures and emerging ruptures. Weakened from within and standing on ground that cannot be wholly stable, a building never has the absolute solid independence that we so desire for our constructions. Deconstruction cannot be split from construction; human culture, motivated by a desire for an unrealizable world of perfect harmony, will always be a process of stabilizing and destabilizing constructions.

Derrida exploited architecture as a trope in his work on construction/deconstruction exactly because the built environment is unthinkable without space and materiality, yet is shaped by discourse that seems immaterial.[v] Deconstruction has been used extensively by contemporary critics who have examined the apparently cohesive "ground" of cultural representations for inner contradictions and critiqued their claims to truth in scores of texts, films, paintings, buildings and all manner of artefacts. Such critiques often appear to lead to nihilism: what is left for human culture when construction is doomed to failure from the start?

But deconstruction only leads to nihilism if our goal remains absolute perfection. Accepting the contingencies of life and the imperfection of every human endeavour leads most of us to continue imagining and creating "better" constructions, which will in turn be deconstructed to make place for even "better" ones. In the judgment of what *constitutes* "better," political discussion comes to the fore. Artworks that allow us, through contemplation and sentient experience, to form reasoned, as well as intuitive, ethical decisions, are a salient part of this discussion.

Josée Dubeau, *Life in a Kite*, 2009

Deconstruction is not rejected in this exhibition but appears, rather, to be taken for granted. *Construction Work* reflects a contemporary waning of the intense focus on deconstruction and a revelling in a new moment of construction. The artists revisit the deconstructive process as if in passing. Dubeau creates a *folly* that subverts the practical functionalism of the house as well as the rationalist principles of the early Modernist architecture that influenced Charles and Ray Eames. Yu's precise, Modernist lines are "crowned" by connected images of scattered sheets of paper. Words on papers blowing away in all directions surely are the epitome of a "destabilized text"! In most of Gilbert's *Le Patrimoine* photographs, it is impossible to distinguish straight photography from manipulated imagery. Rather than using the tactics that many photographers have until recently used to deconstruct photography's claim to veracity – such as making appropriation obvious by including the photographer's shadow to indicate a subjective position – Gilbert displays a cavalier disregard for traditional beliefs in photograph's truthfulness. Taking its deconstruction as a *fait accompli*, she uses Photoshop to make seemingly coherent pictures. A strange juxtaposition of elements, however, betrays her photographs' fissures, even if they are not obvious at first glance.

In *Le Patrimoine*, shacks and buildings, scenic roads and nature trails transform the natural land-scape in a way that goes far beyond the human animal's need for basic food and shelter. A disparate range of québécois cultural icons — a *patate-frite* hut, *coureur de bois* costumes, Krieghoff horse-drawn sleds, figures in snowy landscapes like a Jean-Paul Lemieux painting, picturesque villages, and even the Tigre Géant – are scattered throughout these photographs as ever so many expres-

sions of Québec-*pure-laine* fantasies. There is a slightly nostalgic, Romantic wistfulness in these photos, which Gilbert accentuates with old-fashioned, black-and-white printing. This nostalgia does not go unacknowledged, however: pictures such as *Feeding the Pigeons* (2009) and *Highway 117 North* (2009), show how cultural fantasies affect the materiality of a landscape – scarred here by logging and construction – and displace those who are considered outsiders, people as well as animals.

Gilbert's work has always been marked by strong ecological concerns. Before becoming an artist, she studied environmental biology and forestry at the University of British Columbia. In the 1980s and 1990s, her photographs of devastated clear-cut areas of the province's forests, followed by portraits of tree planters, gained wide recognition.[vi] A former tree planter herself, Gilbert's work was clearly motivated by a desire to expose the exploitation of nature in straight, documentary photographs. Her use of a large-format camera, in the tradition of North American landscape and documentary photography and the early activist landscapes of Ansel Adams, provoked a sense of mourning, not altogether ironic, for the loss of Romantic illusions of an untarnished nature that now cannot even be imagined. Digital manipulation, which she began to use in 1996, allowed her to be more direct in referencing the passing of time and illuminating the underlying Romantic desires and dreams that gave form to traditional representations of landscape.

Previous pages: Jinny Yu, *Sequence*, 2009. Above: Lorraine Gilbert, *Feeding the Pigeons*, 2009

Above: Lorraine Gilbert, *Highway 117 North*, 2009. Next: *Highway 117 North* (detail)

Lorraine Gilbert, *Landscaping*, 2009

Lorraine Gilbert, *Montagne d'Argent*, 2009

With the exception of *Feeding the Pigeons*, where a huge pile of cut logs dominates the picture plane, the construction sites in *Le Patrimoine* hardly convey the sense of political indignation that we might expect from an eco-centred artist. *Promenade, Afternoon Walk* (not in the exhibition) of 2006, for instance, which depicts a man, woman and child walking down a woodsy trail, appears at first sight to be an idyllic family outing in the country. On second glance, we begin to notice the snow fence, the stone wall leading up the hill to what may be a house under construction, and then the man's hard hat. All these signs of construction blend into the background, not least because they don't belong in the picturesque image we *want* to see.

Like the pedestrians in *Montagne d'Argent* [Silver Mountain] (2009), who barely glance at the para-medics on the road, we see mainly what we desire. The deterioration of the environment passes us by like a "slow catastrophe," to use the artist's words.[vii] We know from scientific reports, reasoned arguments, and the drone of news media that the earth needs saving. But for the most part, our own lives are not in immediate danger and so deeper desires take precedence, desires for spaces in which we can imagine an ultimate harmony between ourselves and our environment. The indifferent by-standers take their Tigre Géant shopping bags home, down the "Rue Privée" [private road], where they can create their own escapist fantasies of paradise.

Gilbert works *with* such desires, rather than dismissing them. *Village* (2009) shows an ideal of a rural Québec community: the church surrounded by white clapboard houses, cows retreating to the shade of the trees on a warm summer day to chew their cud. A wire fence stretches along the foreground of this bucolic scene, as if to keep out elements that could upset its equilibrium. To the right, a pho-tographer focuses on a potential drama: a mother wolf stands inside the enclosure with her pup be-hind her, watching the resting cows with their calves. He is "shooting" wild animal nature from inside a pastoral calendar picture. The dream image of the québécois village is not only reiterated by count-less photographers like this one, weighted down by his gear, but also by developers: several photos in the *Le Patrimoine* series show the resort village of Mont Tremblant, and echo (loudly) the photo of the sleepy hamlet of Saint-Sixte.

The cultural critic and philosopher Walter Benjamin took such dream images as signs of deep-seated and unfulfilled desires that found their expressions in all sorts of common artefacts, conventional ar-chitecture, clichéd nature imagery, cheap printed materials, fairy tales and folk tales.[viii] Gilbert, too, has expressed a love of folk imagery, of corny pictures such as a little house in the woods surrounded by an impossible array of birds and other wildlife.[ix] In *Habitat 2007* (2009) she painstakingly im-plants a number of birds and beavers in close proximity to each other. Like Benjamin, Gilbert does not reject such "dream-images" as pure nostalgia. Benjamin recognized them as "ur"-signs that could be re-imagined in a utopia that, in his words, "…has left its trace behind in a thousand config-urations of life from permanent buildings to ephemeral fashions."[x]

In *Le Patrimoine* such traces of utopia can be found in dreamt-of pastoral landscapes, but also in the dream of a homeland. Like magic spells in an adventurous fairy tale, Gilbert sprinkles icons of Québec's cultural history throughout the photographs. *Frites du Loup* (2009) places "pioneers," hunting and

Lorraine Gilbert, *Le Patrimoine* (2006–)

Lorraine Gilbert, *Habitat 2007*, 2009

Lorraine Gilbert, *Frîtes du Loup*, 2009

cutting wood, near a *patate-frite* shack that signifies a more contemporary "typical Québécois" way of finding provisions. In *Open Water* (2009), the landscape becomes a snowy, but dangerous, fairy land, with horse-drawn sleighs and intrepid heroes undaunted by the black, swirling water. As humorous as these out-of-place icons are, they do not add up to a "homeland": their presence thus cautions the viewer not to think of "le patrimoine" as naturally grounded in the land. Gilbert deconstructs the concept of "homeland" as a natural given, but re-positions it as a wish-image that signifies the desire for an ultimate state of plenitude – forever deferred – that will finally feel like "home."

Home as a metaphor for the ultimate utopia prevails in the writing of the German philosopher Ernst Bloch (1885-1977). He kept utopian thought alive in a time when Nazism twisted its spirit to condone violent coercion as a necessary means to an indisputable, prescribed end. In his thought, while we long for *Heimat* (home, homeland) – a term he deliberately conscripted from the Nazis – we cannot imagine what it looks like. Longing for a divine realm is part of human consciousness but this realm

is forever removed in time, and it cannot be named or otherwise represented. Yet Bloch was well aware that it is impossible to dream of a better world without letting the imagination turn to concrete places. We find, according to Bloch, a "Vor-schein," an "anticipatory illumination," in the art and religion of the present and the past, which gives us a glimmer, an outline, of the final castle-in-the-sky.[xi]

Bloch was criticized for using the concept of home as a universal metaphor for the ultimate utopia, rather than describing it as the product of centuries of wishful creations, an accumulation of real and fictional gratifications of the past.[xii] But although it is true that the idea of home is historically determined, home as a place of refuge is a recurring narrative theme in utopian tales that range from Atlantis to El Dorado. Hope for a better future often finds a concrete outlet in the will to construct

Lorraine Gilbert, *Open Water*, 2009

better homes. In the insecure Europe of the 1920s and 1930s, longing for a better world is expressed in the idealist dreams of the Constructivists in Russia, De Stijl in The Netherlands, the German Bauhaus, and the singular visions of Le Corbusier in France. Everywhere in the Western world, countless plans were produced to redesign cities and erect affordable functional homes with new industrial materials.

Insecure times are here again. Whereas architecture is a topic of interest to many contemporary artists, it is usually the entropy of Modernist ideals that holds the attention of painters such as Canada's Alison Norlen and Martin Golland, the German Matthias Weischer, and the Dutch Tjebbe Beekman. In contrast, the architecture-inspired works of Dubeau and Yu look toward the future by revealing some of the ideals that underpin Modernist architecture and that could be worth redeeming.

Josée Dubeau's *Life in a Kite* may show an affinity for Modernist ideals, but her appreciation has only gradually been sifted from an ongoing critical investigation of Modernist architecture's homogeneity and anonymity. Modular building, once the answer to the need for cheap, functional and fast construction for growing populations in war-ravaged cities, has become a cancer, metastasized to all urban centres of the world. Dubeau began her geometric, volumetric constructions at the Künstlerhaus Bethanien in Berlin (2004-05). There she outlined generic office furniture – desks, seats, shelving and filing cabinets – with lengths of thin pine rods. Her life-size, three-dimensional "drawings in space" created a virtual office space in which people could circulate. *Espacement* [Spacing] (2005) was the first in a series of installations that critiqued the standardized construction and interior design of our era. By stripping furniture of its mass, colour and texture, she emphasized the sameness of these objects, which reflect and serve the uniformity of a globalized organisation of human societies. As she has written: "The reduction of these sculptures down to contour lines describes more than a model of organisation: it reveals the underlying uniformity that bureaucracy is introducing."[xiii]

In subsequent installations such as *Bachelor* (2006) and *Suburbia* (2007), she deconstructed ideas of personal taste and sense of place in a mechanized world of corporate production. Their three-dimensional outlines not only dematerialized the objects but showed the basic sameness of modern design. "If everything looks the same everywhere," she has observed, "then everywhere becomes 'nowhere', thereby generating an indifferent continuous space."[xiv] In *Dédoublement* [Doubling] (2008), Dubeau made walls with "building blocks" created out of pine rods, which measure 10" x 10" x 7'. Multiplying these modules into the hundreds, Dubeau reused them in *Life in a Kite* to create an installation that looks at the optimistic aspirations of mid-twentieth-century American architecture, which in turn had looked back at early Modernist architecture of the 1920s and 1930s.

The Case Study House Program was instigated by *Arts & Architecture* magazine in 1945 as a way to develop detached homes for new families of soldiers returning from the war. Although inspired by Modernism, many of the architects of the Case Study Houses transformed the codes of the International Style, experimenting with different materials and adapting to the needs and possibilities of the time. Thomas Hine, a writer on the history of design, comments: "Their matter-of-fact attitude

Josée Dubeau, *Life in a Kite*, 2009

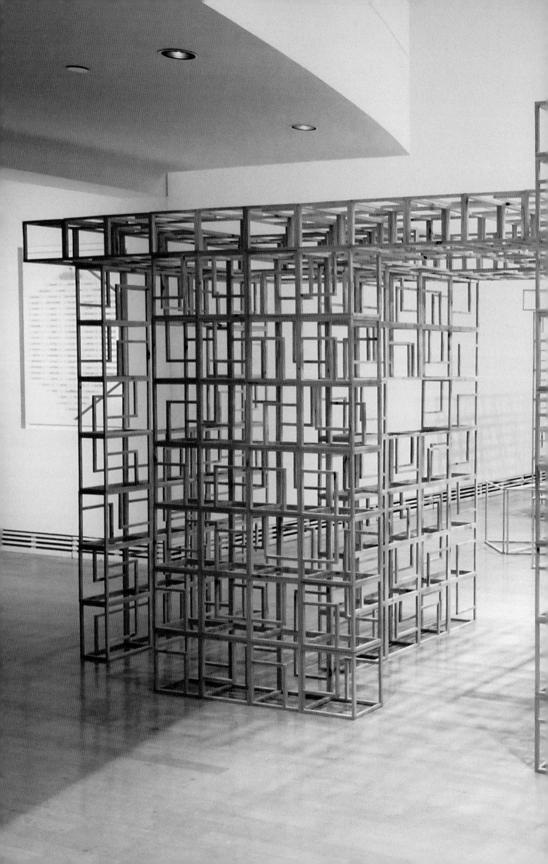

toward technology and their generally practical, middle-class Modernism reflected a more general postwar willingness to start new and figure out what works."[xv]

Dubeau was attracted by a little hand-drawn sketch that Charles and Ray Eames had made for their Case Study House (number 8), showing two box-like, flat-roofed buildings – a house and a studio – erected from lightweight steel and glass, much like a Meccano set. It was featured in *Architectural Forum* (September 1950) with the title "Life in a Chinese Kite."[xvi] Inspired by the Eames's playful attitude and sharing their interest in box kites, Dubeau created *Life in a Kite* in homage to the innovative designer couple.

Life in a Kite could be read as a deconstruction of Modernist architecture just as much as Dubeau's earlier installations, but its title and her stated intent to honour the Eames House shifts the work into a more constructive moment.[xvii] Here, by stripping a building of everything but its outlines, she signifies her ambivalence to its underlying sameness: the emptiness becomes openness to endless spatial possibilities, a play of construction and reconstruction. The Eameses were avid collectors of kites and designed construction toys for children, most famously The Toy, manufactured in 1950. It consisted of lightweight geometric panels and dowels that could be connected to make a tent, a boat, a house, or whatever suited the children's play: constructions that resembled kites as well as the Eames House.[xviii] Dubeau's *Life in a Kite* never pretends to be anything other than a playful but serious folly. Serious, because imagining life in a kite helps us to move away from the idea of the house as an impermeable shell that separates us from our environment. The openness of her installation, like the Eames House, suggests a space of connections, an opening up towards the outside and a flow towards the other.

But a house like a kite also signifies a longing for a utopian place of utter freedom. To be free from unstable foundations and no longer affected by the shifting ground, life in a kite rises above embodied existence and its inevitable deterioration. It is this longing for transcendence that connects Dubeau's installation with the verticality of Yu's two-dimensional *Sequence.*

Even without knowledge of the reference to Le Corbusier's Dominican Monastery of Sainte-Marie de La Tourette, Yu's thin, vertical lines, which echo the gallery's pillars, speak to *architecture*'s lofty erections, the awe-inspiring heights of cathedrals and towering high-rises alike. The lines reach and touch the modular "frieze" of the chaotic blown-paper scenes above them, quickly deconstructing any suggestions of rationalist planning of utopia. But the rhythmic sequence of the lines – like notes in a musical score – prompts a further investigation into the meaning of their source. The lines form a scaled down but precise recreation of one of La Tourette's fenestration patterns. The long and narrow windows of the south and west façades of the famous monastery appear to extend the building's *pilotis*, Le Corbusier's signature stilts that lift his buildings off the ground.[xix]

Like Gilbert and Dubeau, Yu does not openly acknowledge her appropriations, taking the sampling of representations as a given in our image-saturated society. She considers herself a nomadic artist, "continuously shifting from one context to the other... slipping in and out of identifiable political and cultural affiliations."[xx] Yu has not visited La Tourette, but in a media age, "nomadic" extends to the virtual realm; even without our seeing the authentic sites or objects, images get ensconced in our conscious or subconscious minds. [xxi] There they lose part or all of their original framing and wait to be reframed in new authentic narratives.

In the original building, the lines of La Tourette signify a spiritual quest: they extend the vertical "legs" that awkwardly hold the monastery in balance on its sloping site. Their upward movement is stopped by a two-storey, overhanging grid of small monks' cells whose windows are darkened by enclosed balconies. La Tourette expresses a longing to become free of the impediment of nature, to attain divine infinity. Described by many as a spiritual place, yet physically uncomfortable and demanding, the building embodies a desire for cosmic unity, while its complex layout and the mysterious play of light and dark on its façade tangibly represent temporal and spatial obstructions that ultimately block this desire's fulfilment.[xxii]

In the white cube of the gallery, the lines retain their transcendental reach, but here the struggle with nature is eliminated; they soar upwards, as if no longer in need of foundations. Meeting the floor of the gallery at a clean, 90-degree angle, they could be contemplated as a pure geometric abstraction, detached in our minds not only from their support but also from their source in La Tourette, and ultimately, from nature. Abstracting the universal from the particular is an exercise in imagining pure objectivity, a divine space without contingencies. It speaks of a spiritual impulse that recurs in Yu's

Jinny Yu, *Sequence*, 2009

paintings. In a previous series, *Story of a Global Nomad*, she isolated and overlaid geometric patterns appropriated from divergent cultures to create abstract, meditative fields.[xxiii] In *Sequence,* however, the lines stand alone in a precise mathematical order that shows an affinity for Le Corbusier's love of harmony, "animated" as he felt it was, "by a single force: the sense of the divine."[xxiv]

In the lives of monks a sense of the divine is obtained through withdrawal from the everyday, through the penance of living in uncomfortable spaces and the wearing of habits of rough cloth so as never to forget the struggle to overcome nature. At La Tourette, Le Corbusier's vertical fenestration lines are stopped by the heavy horizontal line of the darkened monks' cells. In contrast, the lines of *Sequence* meet a frieze that is light and chaotic in feeling. In it, we see a loosely painted figure to the right, standing on a quay, who has just released or lost a stack of papers that is blown high into the air, over the water and amongst cars and people. The white of the fluttering sheets of paper dominates the image, catching the light reflected off the painting's aluminum support, which shines through the dark background in places. Taken from a scene Yu remembered from a movie she found otherwise forgettable, the aluminium frieze and painted lines form an odd juxtaposition of sources and imagery that would have pleased the surrealist in Le Corbusier.[xxv]

The fluttering papers are as far removed from the concept of a solid building as one can get. Their trajectory is like the nomad's – dependent on peoples' whims and cruelty and the capriciousness of wind and water. Any new construction, the frieze suggests, needs to be attuned to the outside, open to the other. Working with the flux of nature, opening oneself up to the endless possibilities of the outside, appears here as the inevitable starting point.

Sequence shows Yu's affinity for Le Corbusier's spiritual aspirations, but the frieze implicitly questions his dominating stance toward the environment. The painting challenges Le Corbusier's sequencing, ordering compulsion; although nature came to play an important role in his thinking, particularly during the 1930s and 1940s, order remained paramount, even over organic systems.[xxvi] Yu's frieze mirrors the fluidity of contemporary nomadic life and declares openness to everyday chance, to disaster as well as to life's possibilities.

A return to the drawing board, as the works of the artists in *Construction Work* suggest, does not mean a total disconnection from history. What can be reconfigured from past constructions is an underlying longing for harmony. Gilbert deconstructs the Romantic naturalism of a "homeland," Dubeau recognizes the vulnerability of Modernist architecture's ideals to corporate exploitation, and Yu criticizes the Modernist indulgence, exemplified by Le Corbusier's work, of taking man as the measure of all things. But for each artist, constructive ideas take precedence over deconstructions. From the unstable, deconstructed premises of Modernism and Romanticism, the artists build new constructions. *Construction Work* reveals that the compulsion to make a paradise on earth continues to spring from a deep human desire to prefigure the Divine, to approximate in the here and now that forever deferred utopian place where all needs and wants, all differences, are dissolved.

NOTES

i   Le Corbusier, *The Modulor: A Harmonious Measure to the Human Scale, Universally Applicable to Architecture and Mechanics* (1954) (Basel/Boston: Birkhäuser, 2000), 74.

ii Elizabeth A.T. Smith, *Blueprints for Modern Living: History and Legacy of the Case Study Houses* (Cambridge, Massachusetts: The MIT Press, 1989).

iii Media release for the exhibition, 23 February 2009.

iv Jacques Derrida, *Of Grammatology* (1967), Trans. Gayatri Spivak (Baltimore. Maryland: Johns Hopkins University Press, 1976).

v   See Mark Wigley, *The Architecture of Deconstruction: Derrida's Haunt* (Cambridge, Massachusetts: The MIT Press, 1993). On pp. 124-25 of *Aspiring to the Landscape: On Painting and the Subject of Nature* (Toronto: University of Toronto Press, 2006), I have discussed Wigley's interpretation of Derrida's construction/deconstruction process more fully.

vi See Gilbert's website < http://ca.geocities.com/lorraine-gilbert@rogers.com/ >, accessed 12 May 2009.

vii Personal communication with the artist, 13 May 2009.

viii Susan Buck-Morss, *The Dialectics of Seeing, Walter Benjamin and the Arcades Project* (Cambridge, Massachusetts and London, England: The MIT Press, 1989), 111-120.

ix Personal communication with the artist, 13 May 2009.

x   Walter Benjamin, as quoted in Buck-Morss, *The Dialectics of Seeing*, 114.

xi Ernst Bloch, *The Utopian Function of Art and Literature, Selected Essays,* Trans. Jack Zipes and Frank Mecklenburg (Cambridge, Massachusetts: The MIT Press, 1988), xxxiii. See also Russell Jacoby, *Picture Imperfect: Utopian Thought for an Anti-Utopian Age* (New York: Columbia University Press, 2005).

xii Maynard Solomon, *Marxism and Art* (New York: A.A. Knopf, 1973), 572-573.

xiii See < www.joseedubeau.com >, accessed 22 May 2009.

xiv Ibid.

xv Thomas Hine, "The Search for the Postwar House" in Smith, *Blueprints for Modern Living*, 167.

xvi See Tamar Zinguer, "Toy," in Beatriz Colomina et al. (eds)., *Cold War Hothouses: Inventing Postwar Culture, from Cockpit to Playboy* (New York: Princeton Architectural Press, 2004), 143-167. The picture is reproduced on p. 148.

xvii Personal communication with the artist, 22 May 2009.

xviii Zinguer, "Toy," 143-167.

xix For images, go to < www.scholarsresource.com/browse/work/2144568143 >, accessed 8 June 2009.

xx Jinny Yu, "Mediation in Abstraction," paper presented at the Universities Art Association of Canada, University of Waterloo, 3 November 2007.

xxi Personal communication with the artist, 6 May 2009.

xxii Alberto Pérez-Gómez and Louise Pelletier, *Architectural Representation and the Perspective Hinge* (Cambridge, Massachusetts and London, England: The MIT Press, 1997), 361-368.

xxiii For images and analyses see *Jinny Yu: Story of a Global Nomad* (Montréal: Éditions Art Mûr and Ottawa: University of Ottawa Press, 2008).

xxiv Le Corbusier, *The Modulor*, 74.

xxv The movie is *Wonder Boys* (2000), directed by Curtis Hanson.

xxvi See Charles Jencks, *Le Corbusier and the Continual Revolution in Architecture* (New York: Monacelli Press, 2000), 225.

WORKS EXHIBITED

JOSÉE DUBEAU

Life in a Kite (2009)
pine wood
Collection of the artist

LORRAINE GILBERT

Le Patrimoine series
inkjet prints, edition 1/5
Collection of the artist

For Sale (2006)
Mont-Tremblant, Québec

Going Places (2006)
Mont-Tremblant, Québec

Sunbathers (2006)
Sainte-Véronique, Québec

Chairlift / Late shift (2009)
Mont-Tremblant, Québec

Feeding the pigeons (2009)
Sainte-Véronique, Québec

Frites du Lac (2009)
Mont-Laurier, Québec

Frites du Loup (2009)
Bréboeuf, Québec

Giant Tiger (2009)
Masson-Angers, Québec

Habitat 2007 (2009)
Mont-Tremblant, Québec

Highway 117 North (2009)
Québec

Hotel (2009)
Mont-Tremblant, Québec

Landscaping (2009)
Mont-Tremblant, Québec

Montagne d'Argent (2009)
Highway 117 North, Québec

Open Water (2009)
Bréboeuf, Québec

Trilliums (2009)
Thurso, Québec

Village (2009)
Saint-Sixte, Québec

JINNY YU

Sequence (2009)
oil on aluminum,
latex paint on wall
Collection of the artist

BIOGRAPHIES

JOSÉE DUBEAU has an MFA in Fine Arts from the University of Québec in Montréal (1994). Her sculptures, drawings and videos are developed in the context of residencies and exhibitions in Canada and abroad, including the IAAB/Christoph Merian Stiftung in Basel (1998), the Internationales Künstlerhaus Villa Concordia in Bamberg, Germany (2002-03), and the Künstlerhaus Bethanien in Berlin (2004-05). In 2009 she was in residence at the Studio of Tokyo in Roppongi Hills, where she was the recipient of grants from the Ministère des relations internationales du Québec, the Conseil des arts et des lettres du Québec, and the Ministère de la Culture, des Communications et de la Condition féminine du Québec. Dubeau's work has been shown at many venues, including the Diefenbunker in Carp, Ontario, Axenéo7 and Daïmôn in Gatineau, the Ottawa Art Gallery and Galerie SAW Gallery in Ottawa, and Skol, Circa, and Occurrence in Montréal. She has received numerous grants from the Canada Council for the Arts. Her work is found in the collection of the Musée National des beaux-arts du Québec and in private collections throughout Ontario, Québec, Switzerland and Germany. She teaches drawing and sculpture at the University of Ottawa.

LORRAINE GILBERT is an Assistant Professor in the Department of Visual Arts at the University of Ottawa, where she has taught since 1990. She has an MFA in Visual Arts from Concordia University (1989) and a B.Sc. from McGill University (1978). Her recent solo exhibitions include *Shaping the New Forest* (Thunder Bay Art Gallery, 2006), *Flora and Fauna* (Karsh-Masson Gallery, Ottawa, 2006), and *Lorraine Gilbert: Selected Works* (Nelson Gallery, University of California at Davis, 2005). Her photographs have been featured in many group exhibitions since 1979, including, most recently, *Global Nature*, a 2009–11 touring exhibition (with Sarah Anne Johnson) organized by the Canadian Museum of Contemporary Photography, and *The Tree: From the Sublime to the Social* (Vancouver Art Gallery, 2008). Gilbert's work is included in the collections of the National Gallery of Canada, Dalhousie Art Gallery, Vancouver Art Gallery, City of Ottawa, Canada Council Art Bank, and Carleton University Art Gallery. She was the recipient in 2003 of the Yousef and Malak Karsh Award from the City of Ottawa and an "A" grant from the Canada Council for the Arts, the latter in direct support of the photographs presented in *Construction Work*. Lorraine Gilbert wishes to thank the Canada Council and Carleton University Art Gallery for their support of her work.

PETRA HALKES is a painter and unaffiliated scholar and curator. She has a Ph.D. from Leiden University in The Netherlands (2001). Her focus is on the persistence of archaic phenomena in visual art as well as in the culture at large, such as religion, the myth of Arcadia, the skills of painting and landscape representation. She has written many catalogue essays and writes regularly for Canadian magazines. Her book, *Aspiring to the Landscape: On Painting and the Subject of Nature*, was published by the University of Toronto Press in 2006. She presented a paper on religion in the work of Komar & Melamid at the 32nd Congress of the International Committee of the History of Art in Melbourne (2008), for which she received a Getty scholarship. Recent curatorial projects include *Mannish: Michael Harrington and Wyn Geleynse* at the Ottawa Art Gallery (2009) and *Barbara Gamble: Natural Affinities* (2008) at the Canadian Museum of Nature.

JINNY YU is an Associate Professor in the Department of Visual Arts at the University of Ottawa. She has an MFA in Visual Arts from York University and an MBA from the Schulich School of Business (2002). Her recent solo exhibitions include *Story of a Global Nomad* (Galerie Art Mûr, Montréal, 2008) and *Ceiling Painting* (Axenéo7, Gatineau, 2008). Her work has also been featured in group exhibitions such as *Breathing Out* (TEAF09, Ulsan City, South Korea, 2009), *Venice: City of Dreams?* (Sotheby's, London, 2007), *Tende a infinito* (Fondazione Bevilacqua La Masa, Venice, 2006), and *Neo Vessel* (Kyoto Municipal Museum of Art, Japan, 2004). Yu was artist-in-residence at the Banff Centre for the Arts, at Stiftung Starke in Berlin, and at Red Gate Gallery in Beijing. Her work is included in the collections of the Musée National des beaux-arts du Québec, City of Ottawa, and Mills Foundation (Montréal), and she is represented by Galerie Art Mûr in Montréal.

CONSTRUCTION WORK

This publication accompanies the exhibition *Construction Work: Josée Dubeau, Lorraine Gilbert, Jinny Yu*, curated by Sandra Dyck and presented at Carleton University Art Gallery from 23 February – 12 April 2009.

Legal deposit – Library and Archives Canada, 2010

ISBN 978-0-7709-0537-8

cuag Carleton University Art Gallery

St. Patrick's Building, Carleton University
1125 Colonel By Drive
Ottawa, Ontario   K1S 5B6
Telephone: 613.520.2120
Fax: 613.520.4409
cuag.carleton.ca

STAFF
Director: Diana Nemiroff
Curator: Sandra Dyck
Collection/Exhibition Assistant: Patrick Lacasse
Administrative Assistant: Alisdair MacRae

CREDITS
Graphic design: Studio:Blackwell, Toronto
Photography: Stephen Fenn; Lorraine Gilbert (pp. 16-17, p. 31)
Printed in Canada by Solisco Tri-Graphic

This publication is supported generously by Carleton University, the Canada Council for the Arts, and the Ontario Arts Council, an agency of the government of Ontario.

Library and Archives Canada Cataloguing in Publication

Construction Work : Josée Dubeau, Lorraine Gilbert, Jinny Yu
Sandra Dyck, curator ; Petra Halkes, guest essayist.

Includes bibliographical references. Catalogue of an exhibition held at Carleton University Art Gallery, Feb. 23 to April 12, 2009.

1. Dubeau, Josée, 1959- --Exhibitions. 2. Gilbert, Lorraine, 1955- --Exhibitions. 3. Yu, Jinny, 1976- --Exhibitions. 4. Art, Canadian--21st century--Exhibitions. I. Dyck, Sandra, 1966- II. Halkes, Petra III. Dubeau, Josée, 1959- IV. Yu, Jinny, 1976- V. Gilbert, Lorraine, 1955- VI. Carleton University Art Gallery

N6545.6.C68 2009   709.71'07471384   C2009-906424-3